EVERNOTE

The Ultimate EVERNOTE ESSENTIALS Guide To Master: Productivity, Time Management, Procrastination, And Goal Setting

3rd Edition

M.J. Brown

Disclaimer

This document is geared towards providing exact and reliable information in regards to the topic and issue covered. The publication is sold with the idea that the publisher is not required to render accounting, officially permitted, or otherwise, qualified services. If advice is necessary, legal or professional, a practiced individual in the profession should be ordered.

- From a Declaration of Principles which was accepted and approved equally by a Committee of the American Bar Association and a Committee of Publishers and Associations.

The information provided herein is stated to be truthful and consistent, in that any liability, in terms of inattention or otherwise, by any usage or abuse of any policies, processes, or directions contained within is the solitary and utter responsibility of the recipient reader. Under no circumstances will any legal responsibility or blame be held against the publisher for any reparation, damages, or monetary loss due to the information herein, either directly or indirectly.

The information herein is offered for informational purposes solely, and is universal as so. The presentation of the information is without contract or any type of guarantee assurance.

The trademarks that are used are without any consent, and the publication of the trademark is without permission or backing by the trademark owner. All trademarks and brands within this book are for clarifying purposes only and are the owned by the owners themselves, not affiliated with this document.

TABLE OF CONTENTS

INTRODUCTION

I want to thank you and congratulate you for purchasing the book, *"EVERNOTE – The Ultimate EVERNOTE ESSENTIALS Guide To Master: Productivity, Time Management, Procrastination, And Goal Setting"*.

This book contains a step-by-step guide to master life management using Evernote, the greatest productivity and management tool ever created and the best thing since sliced bread!

Our lives are complex and chaotic at the best of times. It is surprising that a lot of us find it acceptable that a business or an organization requires management but never think of applying management to our lives. Those of us, who have tried to manage our life like a business, have found how hard it can be. That's where Evernote comes in.

Think of Evernote as an external memory, like a USB hard disk, that plugs into your brain. This additional bit of brain can store information in any form and also help you retrieve it quickly. The simplicity and freedom of use of Evernote make it a powerful tool in the right hands. With a little bit of creativity and a little bit of knowledge about the tricks of Evernote you can master life management.

3 PARTS

Part 1 will teach you the basics of Evernote. Beginning from installation and account setup, we'll go through all the basic utility of Evernote such as creating notes, creating notebooks, searching, syncing etc.

In **Part 2** we'll dig deeper into Evernote and some advanced strategies that will help you fall in love with Evernote. When you learn these advanced tricks, you can experience Evernote fully and see how well it can work.

In **Part 3** you will learn about how to use Evernote to manage your life. This part will teach you how to best use Evernote and also teach you a few tricks about life management. Life management is a very personal thing and I don't claim to have any universal system that will work for everyone. But I will teach you the basics and give you the ideas that will help you create your own life management system built around Evernote.

Thanks again for purchasing this book, I hope you enjoy it!

M.J. Brown

PART ONE

- Evernote Basics -

Chapter 1: Introduction to Evernote

S imply put, Evernote is a management tool that allows you to capture, store, organize and recall all kinds of information. Every piece of information is called a note but a note can be absolutely anything. It can be a picture, a video clip, audio clips, a handwritten note, long form text, emails, text captured from the web, blog posts, tweets, recipes etc.

Any and every piece of information, whether it is online, offline, or just in your head, can be captured and stored in Evernote. Can you imagine how powerful this can be?

In his book, *Getting Things Done*, productivity author David Allen talks about the idea of having a ubiquitous capture list. A list that contains every thought and idea that pops into your head. Evernote is ubiquitous capture meets cloud technology.

When you have all these ideas and To Do lists in your head it can overwhelm you. It can cause you a lot of stress, as you constantly wonder if you are forgetting something. Your brain keeps reminding you of tasks that are to be done next week, making the tasks you are doing right now, harder to execute. By capturing all your thoughts and ideas in one place, you can empty your head of all the clutter and focus on what's important. You will no longer be constantly distracted by random thoughts that feel urgent.

By capturing all the information in one place you can feel assured that you are not missing anything. You have your tasks to do for the day and you can go about doing them to the best of your ability. It reduces stress and increases productivity. Overall it helps in managing your day to day and long-term life.

Evernote does this brilliantly by providing you one place to store all information that enters your head. That's not all; Evernote offers you the capability to capture this information from any device, from any place, at any time. You can use Evernote on your laptop or desktop computer, on your phone, on your tablet and even on devices you don't own through the web browser version of Evernote.

This means that no matter where you are, you can store information in your account on Evernote. All the information is stored in the cloud so you can access it from multiple devices. Even if you are not connected to the internet, you can capture information and when the device goes online, Evernote will automatically sync the new information and it will be available to you on all your other devices.

You can capture information from one device and view it on another. You can make notes at home and view them at work. Your ubiquitous capture list goes wherever you go.

There were similar tools around when Evernote came along in 2008, but Evernote does, everything you want from such a data and information managing tool, and more. This has made it the most popular tool for productivity nerds today. Developers are making apps that add on to the functionality of Evernote making it better and better every day.

Evernote is available as free software with a premium membership plan at $5 per month or $45 per annum. The premium account offers you the ability to upload more data per month along with a few advanced features. The free version is just as powerful and provides a lot of value. This is why Evernote grew to 11 million users in its first 3 years and 100 million users in the next 3!

If you are serious about improving management, increasing productivity and becoming successful then you can't ignore Evernote any longer. It is an easy to use tool with a very short learning curve. In this book you will learn not just the basics but also the advanced uses of Evernote and how you can improve and manage your life with it. So read on and remember to follow along with the steps so you get firsthand experience of every step.

But before we delve into the wonderful world of the note, let us have a small look at why purchasing it will help you in doing your bit for the environment.

The biggest gain from purchasing this app is that you will be able to cut out all paper from your life.

From schools to offices, people would use papers to take down notes, prepare files, presentation, record data etc. Desks would overflow with these papers and one could hardly spot a free space, not to mention the amount of dust that these would cause. I am sure you are experiencing headaches just by visualizing these.

But with the Evernote app, this very problem can be effectively dealt with. People can do all of the above, without having to ever make use of a piece of paper.

You can easily scan all your existing documents and do away with the hard copies. Yes that is right, you can effectively get rid of everything that is in your house, on your desk etc. and cluttering your personal space. Will it not be simply superb to have something that will effectively get rid of all the clutter in your office and home? That is exactly why the ever note app is popular and sure to make you extremely happy.

You can do away with tons and tons of your paper and, in fact, recycle it to make something useful. That way, you will be contributing to the environment. Not only will you do away with the paper but also not litter it. You will recycle and use it for better things. If you use less paper then you will also help conserve the environment in a big way.

You will eliminate the hindrance of messy desks, dusty drawers and heavy college bags. Aren't these what give you nightmares? You will now have the chance to get rid of all this and remain as organized as possible. You will not have to worry about any of the unwanted papers and other things disturbing you when you wish to operate smoothly in your work and personal space.

You will also effectively save on a lot of time, as you will not have to skim through piles and piles of papers, just to find a small piece of information. You can simply type in the name and find the file or data. Imagine trying to do that with sheets of paper, will it be possible? Here, all you have to do is type in the name of the file and find it with ease. You don't have to run around looking for the pile, look for the pages etc.

You can also successfully carry just your phone or notebook to a meeting or presentation and avoid a heavy bag containing tons of papers and documents. This means that you get a chance to travel light as well. You don't have to worry about having to carry many things with you when you travel, especially papers, and have all of it in your phone or tablet. Doesn't that sound simply delightful?

You can also carry lists while you shop, soft copies of bills and receipts etc. you won't have to worry about misplacing a bill and not finding it to return something back. You will have the chance to carry all your bills and receipts and not worry about not having any at any time.

These form all the personal benefits that you can avail from leading a life free of paper, now let us shed some light on the environmental benefits.

By adopting the Evernote, you help conserve the environment and reduce the number of trees that will be cut down. You will help future generations have a greener and better tomorrow. You will not have to worry about not having enough trees in the future.

With more trees, there will be more oxygen and a better environment can be established. Isn't that what you want for your children? Do you really want to exhaust everything by using it for yourself and not keep anything for children? I don't think so!

You will help welcome a greener and cleaner tomorrow for your kids, and they will be able to lead healthier lives, which is what any parent would want for their child.

You will also effectively help in reducing the amount of clutter, as you will not keep throwing out piles and piles of paper. Paper pollution is now probably the most viral of all and you can easily cut down on it just by taking up ever note.

Installation

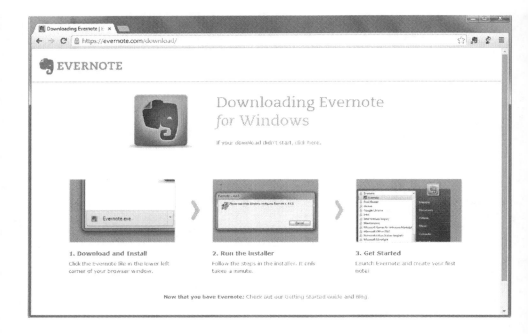

The first step of course, is to download and install Evernote. You can do so from their website, http://evernote.com/download/. The website will automatically detect your device and download the appropriate software. You can download Evernote on your PC, MAC, iPhone, iPad, Android phones, Blackberry or Windows phone. This book will work with Evernote for Windows but the process is similar for all devices and once you get the hang of it you should be able to install and use Evernote on all of your devices.

When you click the link, an installer will download on to your computer. The installer is an .exe or executable file. Double click on the .exe file and it will show a security warning.

Click "Run" to launch the installer. It will then ask you some basic questions such as accepting the license agreement and choosing where to install the software.

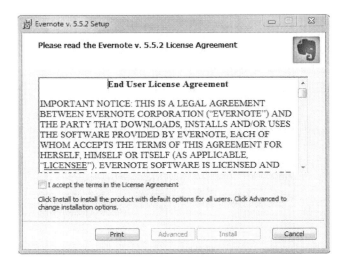

It is pretty straightforward and once you go through the options you should see the installing screen below.

It will take a few minutes to finish the installation and you don't have to do anything except wait till the following screen shows up.

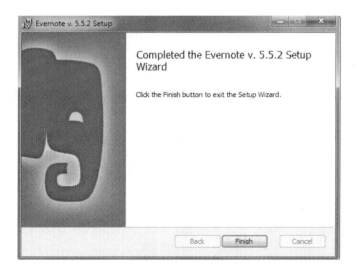

This means that the installation is complete and when you click on "Finish" you will see the following screen.

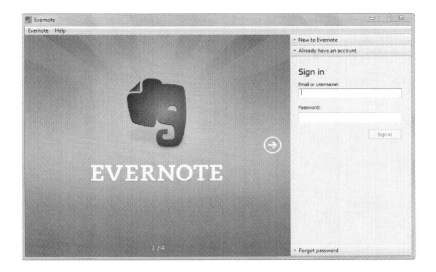

As you can see you need to sign in to your account. If you are a new user and don't have an account yet, you need to click on the "New to Evernote" link and create a new account.

Creating an account is free and simple to do. You just need to enter your email id and create a password. Once you have your account you can use the information to sign in.

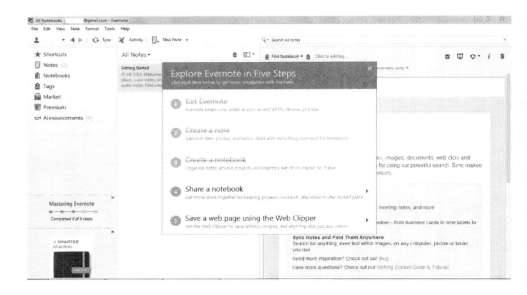

You will then be shown this step by step getting started guide. You can follow along and learn how to create a note, how to create a notebook, how to share your notebooks with others and how to save web pages. For now, if you want, you can skip this, as I'll discuss all this in a short while.

Apart from the website, this is how you can download it on the various other mentioned platforms.

For Android phones and tablets

➢ Download the app from the Google play store.

➢ Login with your Google account or create a new one.

➢ Sync it with your other devices that you want to sync it with. You can also enable the Wi-Fi only syncing by choosing it from the menu option.

➢ To start creating a note, simply tap on the note editor (explained in detail later)

➢ A separate Evernote widget is available for Android users, which is meant to be a handy shortcut to the full app.

➢ The widget is easy to use and you can access features such as New Note, Quick Snapshot, Audio Note, Quick Reminder Page, Camera, Search Settings, Skitch and Speech-to-text Note, all with the touch of a single button.

➢ You can upgrade to premium by paying $5 a month or $45 a year.

For your Mac

➢ You can download the app from the iOS app store.

➢ You can login from your apple account or create a new account.

➢ You can also login with your Google account.

➢ You can the sync it with all your various devices.

➢ You can avail the 2-step verification to increase the security option.

➢ To create a new note, click on the new note button located on the top center of the app window.

➢ Mac does not have a separate widget and the app icon can be placed on the desktop for easy access.

For the iPad, iPod touch and iPhone

➣ Evernote made changes to their previous iOS platform app and the new one is said to be much more advanced and also extremely easy to use.

➣ Once you download it from the App store, you can sign in with your apple account or create a new account and you can also login through your Google account.

➣ You can sync all your different devices. You can either choose the automatic sync option or do a manual sync. The manual sync will only require your approval.

➣ The Evernote widget is not available on these platforms but you can place the icon on the desktop or on the lock screen by choosing Settingsàcontrol center and choosing "Enable Access on Lock Screen".

For windows phone

➣ You can download the app from the windows app store

➣ To create a new note, go to the Home Screen, tap on any of the Quick Notes buttons to create a new blank note, or to start by adding an attachment like a photo, or an audio piece. To enter text, tap into the text area of a note. (explained in detail)

➣ To edit the note, click the standard edit icon of the slant pencil and edit your notes.

➣ There is no separate widget for windows devices either but you can create a shortcut on the desktop.

For windows desktop

➤ You can download the desktop version through your windows app store or install it from the website.

➤ To create a new note, choose the "New note" option located on the top center of the window bar.

➤ To access the sync option on your windows desktop, go to the Toolsàoptions and select the sync tab. Choose an option from the drop down menu and choose whether you want automatic synchronization or manual.

➤ There is no widget that is available but a shortcut can be created on the desktop or dragged and place on the taskbar.

For blackberry users

➤ Download the app from the Blackberry OS store.

➤ To create a new note, choose from the various options including snapshot, upload file, text note and audio note.

➤ You can sync your various devices by choosing the appropriate option.

➤ Blackberry does not have an Evernote widget but you can make a shortcut on your home screen for easy access.

Familiarize

Now that you've installed Evernote let's get familiar with it. This is what the Evernote interface looks like.

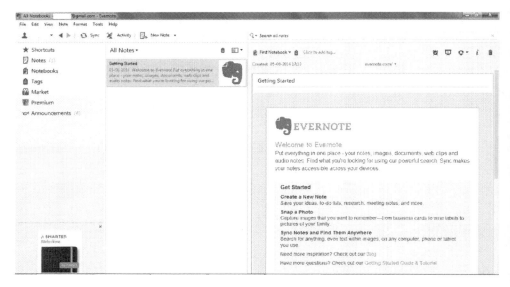

For beginners it might look a little confusing so let's go through each area of this user interface one by one.

The Top Area

The top area has the menu bar, the tool bar and a search box. The menu bar has 7 standard menus that are common to most software applications and you shouldn't have any trouble understanding the menus once you take a bit of time to go through them. The toolbar can be optimized to show the tools you use the most.

The Sidebar

The sidebar is a handy place to get to your notes. It contains a shortcut folder where you can add your most important notes to reach them quickly. You can look for your notes, notebooks and tags from the sidebar and also go to the Evernote Market, upgrade to Premium account and receive Announcements from Evernote. Below these navigation items is a space for notifications and advertisements.

The Note Area

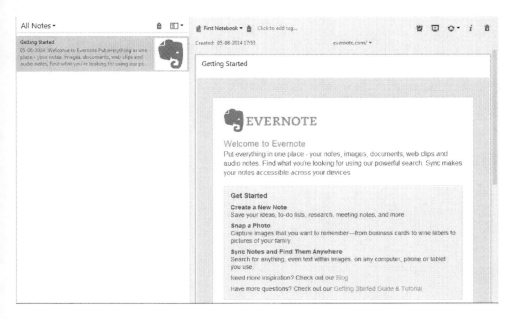

The rest of the area is where you view and edit your notes. The left side is the note list and the right side is the note editor. By default you have a note created for you as the "Getting Started" note. It contains links that will introduce you to the most basic features of Evernote.

If you look closely in the note area you can see some icons on the top right hand corner. These are used to set a reminder with a note, create a presentation, share your notes with others, find out more information about the note and delete the note.

You can arrange the note list by clicking on the organizer icon. You can arrange the notes to be viewed as a list, as snippets or as clips. You can also sort your notes based on various criteria. This ability to organize and quickly search your notes gives Evernote its power as a great productivity tool.

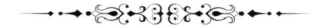

Chapter 2: Master the Basics

I f the last chapter was a bit boring, it's only because it's important to get familiar with the user interface of any software if you want to utilize its full potential. Now that you know where everything is in Evernote, we can move forward and talk about how to use Evernote.

As I said before, Evernote is like an additional memory space that you use to store information so that your own brain remains uncluttered and focused. You don't even have to use your own brainpower to search that information to find what you are looking for.

Creating a Note

This is the very basics of it and everything mostly centers on a note. To begin with, you can start by taking some notes. A note can be absolutely anything. It can be a to do list, a task list for the day, a goals list for your life, a bucket list, a recipe, a draft of your email, even a draft of your novel! It can be pictures of your birthday party, inspiring pictures you found online, a scanned picture from a magazine containing your dream house etc. All your memories can be stored on Evernote. Funny pictures, ideas, snapshots, anything can be turned into a note.

You can also start making a business related note, if you want to use the app for a business purpose.

You can add audio files to your notes as well. Do you remember those voice recorders that shrinks are shown using in so many movies? You can do that on Evernote. You can turn videos into notes as well. The potential is infinite.

To make a new note, just click on the "new note" icon in the toolbar. There are a few other ways to open a new note as well but this is the fastest and easiest. The note will open in the note editor area. You can write and format the text easily from the editor. You can add pictures, audio, files etc.

If you are creating a To Do list you can add checkboxes that can actually be checked off as you do the things on the list. Evernote automatically saves everything you type into the note editor so you don't have to worry about saving.

Give your note a title and add a few tags. Tags will come in handy later, when you have a lot of notes and you want to organize them.

Creating a Notebook

A notebook is a place where notes are stored. It's a folder for all your notes. When you begin with Evernote, there is already a default notebook created for you. When you delete a note, it goes to another default notebook called Trash so you can restore it if you need it later.

To organize your notes nicely, you should create several notebooks. You can create one for work, one for personal life, one for life goals, one for relationships, one for travel etc. In the last part we'll talk about which notebooks to create to manage your life properly.

To create a notebook, just click on "notebooks" in the sidebar and a list of all your notebooks will appear. On the top left hand corner there will be a "+ New Notebook" button which will create a new notebook for you.

To move notes from one notebook to another you can just drag and drop the note into the new notebook. When you drag a note over the notebooks link in the sidebar, all the notebooks will open up in a drop down list and you can drag the note to the desired notebook and drop it there. You can also move or copy notes through the note menu or by right clicking on the note.

Creating a Stack

To help you organize your notes even further you can create notebook stacks. This basically means that you can add similar notebooks in one stack, like subfolders within a folder.

To stack two notebooks together just open the notebooks link on the sidebar and drag and drop one notebook on top of the other. This will create a new stack. You can rename it by right clicking on the stack in the sidebar and clicking "rename". You can add as many notebooks in a stack as you want by simply dragging and dropping.

Stacks will help you organize similar notebooks under one common area.

Editing an Evernote Note

Editing a note is made easy, as you can simply click on it and start to edit it. You need not have to open the note in a separate tab and start editing as and when you have to. Once you are done making the changes you can save it.

Deleting a Note

Deleting a note is extremely easy. You have to simply select the note that you wish to delete and drag and drop it in the trash can. You can also right click on it and select the "delete" option. You can also pick it up, drag it and drop it in the dustbin symbol present on the bottom.

Moving your Evernote Notes to Notebooks

You can organize your various notes by creating a handy notebook. To do so, simply select all the notes that you want to place in the notebook and drag and drop them into it.

Modifying the font

To modify the font, simply click on the toolbar to change the type of font, the color of the font, the font size and the font styles. You will find all the familiar fonts, which are available in MS Word. You can also choose headings and other features such as Bold, Italics and Underlining, just like you would in word.

Modifying the layout

To modify the layout, simply click on the toolbar to align the text or to create a bullet and or a number list. You can also avail all the various options that you will have available on any of the MS products. You can also simply paste content as plain text without any formatting.

In order to simplify the formatting, simply select the "Simplify Formatting" option to create the same format all throughout the note. You can create a unified look and not have to individually change the text in a file.

Adding attachments

It is extremely easy to add your pictures, videos, music etc. You can simply add the file amidst the

To attach a multimedia file simply click on "Record audio", "Take A Snapshot" or "Attach A File" attachment options in the toolbar.

Also, you can create new audio and sound notes by choosing the option from the file menu. The limit on per note attachment size is 25MB for free users and 100MB for premium users.

Storage

Storage is made extremely easy with the Evernote app. One of the main features of the app is to maintain a copy of all your various documents and files. You will be able to have multiple copies, so as to not be worried if you lose one.

The storage feature will help you get rid of the various hardcopies of all your various files and documents. You will be able to have a cleaner and more organized office. And the app is big enough to take a very large load.

And it is conveniently built to allow you to have separate folders for each type of your files including personal, professional and social. You can have as many folders as you like and not get confused between any. You can easily look for a stored file, just by typing in its name in the search option and not have to manually go through piles and piles of paper.

And so, just with the installation of the Evernote app, you can easily and conveniently get rid of papers and have a handy means of storing all your important data.

Shortcuts

A powerful feature in Evernote is the shortcuts section. You can drag and drop any note or notebook or notebook stack in the shortcuts link in the sidebar. This will help you get easy access to the most important notes and notebooks that you use the most.

Reminders

Another important feature is the ability to add reminders to your notes. You can add a reminder by clicking on the clock icon in the note editor area. This will add that particular note in the reminders list. You can add the date on which you want to be reminded of that note. You can schedule meetings and use Evernote as a calendar and scheduler with this option.

You can set an alarm for the reminder, which can be a pop up box that appears on your device at the set time or an email that you receive in the morning of the set date.

Sharing

Once you start creating notes and organize all of your life from one single tool, you should begin to see tremendous results in productivity. But that's not all, you can use Evernote to share your notes with others and communicate ideas in a productive manner.

Sharing is made extremely easy with the Evernote app. The app is designed to allow you to share all your files and documents with extreme ease.

You can share all your data and information seamlessly and with as many people as you like. You can also share data, documents, files etc.

If you do not want to share the entire page then you can simply share portions of it or even, simply copy the URL of a page and share it.

The feature is especially useful, when you are working on a collaboration and need to exchange files in order to work on the same project. You can also share other things such as lists, files, presentations, ideas etc.

You can share your notes even with those who don't use Evernote. You can share your notes on social networks and through email. You can also create shared notebooks to collaborate with those who do use Evernote. They can either view the notes in the notebook or edit them, according to your preference.

And so, if you need to upload any presentation related data to a Facebook page then you can easily do it via the app. You can also share it via twitter or any of the other forms of social media and email.

And if you feel that only a few people must have access to it, then you can selectively make the files and information available. You can choose the number of people that you wish to share the information with. Another feature of the sharing option is that, you can stop sharing your files with others. You can, at any time, simply go to the "Modify Sharing" option and remove the data from public view. You can also, selectively remove the data.

And you can do the sharing from anytime and from anywhere. Suppose you created the note from your phone and it synced with all your other devices, then you can share it from any other device of your choice.

And you need not always share the files alone, you can also share pictures of the files, that you can produce by using the "Skitch" feature and also allow others to use the annotate feature over it.

This makes it the choicest tool to work on a project with people situated anywhere around the world. Any changes they make will appear on your activity feed. You can see the list of shared notes that have been edited recently so you can keep up with the project.

Annotation

You can annotate pictures from within Evernote and really get your ideas across. To annotate any picture just hover the mouse pointer over it and an "annotate" button will appear on the top right hand corner of the picture. By clicking on this link you will open the image editor window and you can choose from the various tools provided to express your ideas.

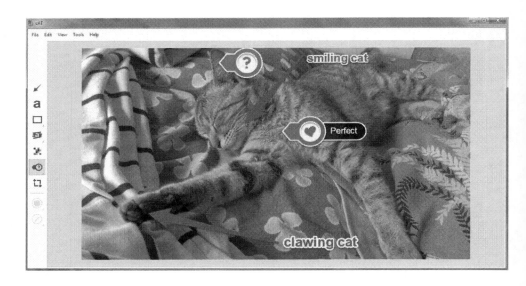

Syncing

When you create a new note, Evernote will automatically sync it to the web server and it will be available on all your devices. You can view it on your computer, phone, tablet, or on a web browser from anywhere in the world.

The auto sync setting is set to sync every 15 minutes but you can change it from tools >> options. You can also choose to manually sync the note by clicking on the sync button in the toolbar. You can use this option after making a major change to a note to make sure that it has been synced.

The true power of Evernote is in this syncing ability so that you can add, edit, share and view all your notes from many different devices and they all stay synced no matter what. So if you get an idea about work while grocery shopping you can just create a quick note from your phone and it will be there when you search for it at work.

The sync function of the app is especially useful for office goers and businessmen. Not to mention for students, who can easily sync their various contents on their various devices. And it not always just be files, it can be pictures, multimedia etc.

And by having such multiple access points, you will be able to successfully run your business smoothly or have a very organized college life.

Let us look at a real life situation to have a better picture: suppose you carried your notebook to class and took down notes. You forgot to carry the notebook home and left it at your college. You can easily avail the notes at home on your pc or your smartphone, as it would have created copies and sent to your various devices.

Similarly, if you forgot your phone at home or your office, then you can retrieve the data from another device that is synced with your mother device.

And so, it is apparent that you will be able to access the various files and data, even if your original device is switched off or even conked.

The sync function will not just aid in not worrying about misplaced devices but also help you save lots of time and effort. The app will make sure that you do not have to rush to find the various transfer devices like USB's and data cables and will do the job for you wirelessly.

And this very feature will help prevent loss of data and files, as unless expressly deleted from the various devices, the files will not be mass deleted. That is to say, if you delete it from your phone by mistake, then it will still be available in your pc and notebook.

The sync feature is also designed to help you make changes and these can be saved on all devices. You can simultaneously save the original as well as the edited copy. This feature is especially useful for students, as they can have multiple edited copies of their notes, projects etc. along with the original ones.

One other important factor for you to note is that, apart from your various synced devices, a copy will also be available with the Evernote servers and so, you can be rest assured of not losing any copy due to accidental deletion.

Searching

Searching for notes becomes important once you have a lot of them. To search just start typing the title of the note, a tag, the name of the notebook or any keyword related to the note. Evernote will automatically suggest search terms for you and you can choose the one you want.

When you enter a word in the search box, Evernote searches not just the notes but also handwritten text within pictures! This feature is only available for premium accounts.

Another good way to search for notes is through the "Atlas" link in the sidebar.

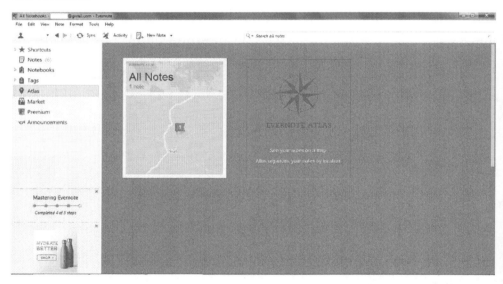

This arranges your notes according to the geo-tags attached to the notes. So if you want to see the notes you made while visiting a particular place you can use atlas. The flags show the number of notes that you have for a particular location. We'll talk about more advanced searching in part 2.

Chapter 3: Evernote Add-Ons

I hope by now you have understood the power of Evernote. The best thing about Evernote is that it doesn't limit you in what you can do and what you can't. Your own creativity sets the limit of how much use you can get out of it. We'll talk about creative ways to use Evernote a little later.

Apart from the basic functions of taking notes and storing information, there are several other add on features that enhance the functionality of Evernote. Let's talk about them now.

Evernote Web Clipper

The Evernote Web Clipper is a browser plug-in that you can download on your computer depending on which browser you use. It helps in turning web pages into notes that automatically get saved in your Evernote account.

You can use this to research web pages. You can save complete pages or just clip certain sections of it. You can also clip an article from the web on your computer and then read it later on your phone or tablet while commuting to work. Anything that inspires you on the internet, whether it is text, images, or links, can be clipped by this plug-in and you can store it in your account and view it anywhere you want. This is explained in detail further in the book.

Evernote Clearly

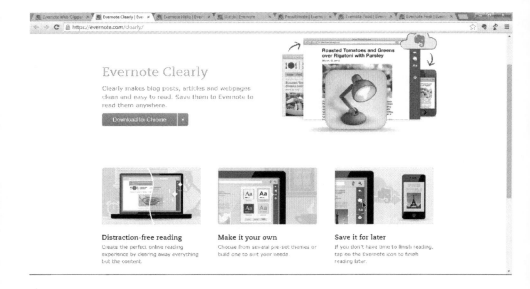

Evernote Clearly is another browser plug-in that helps you surf the net without the usual distractions of advertisements and design features. If you do a lot of reading online, this is a must have tool for you. It will help you stay focused on what you are reading and remove all distractions.

You can create your own themes or choose an existing one to create a visually pleasing minimalistic reading environment. You can also save articles for later and add them to your Evernote account so you can read them from any device at any time. This in fact is extremely useful for students as they can easily access webpages that they have to read without getting distracted by unnecessary things on the internet. So this is a must have for all those that wish to use the internet resourcefully and are not interested in using it for unnecessary things.

Evernote Hello

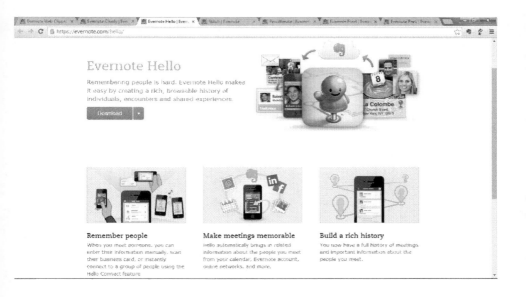

Evernote Hello is a wonderful tool to have if you meet a lot of people and find it hard to remember everyone. This tool lets you create an instant contact card for every person you meet. You can enter information manually or scan their business cards. You can even click a picture from your phone and add it to their account so you have a picture to go with the name. If they are an Evernote user and use the Hello Connect feature, you don't need to add anything and just connect to their group to get all of their information.

Evernote Hello will also search for the new contact in your notes and on the web. It will fetch all information related to that person including their social network accounts and any notes you might have made that are related to them. This is a very powerful option to create a comprehensive history of all your contacts and you'll never forget anything about anyone.

Skitch

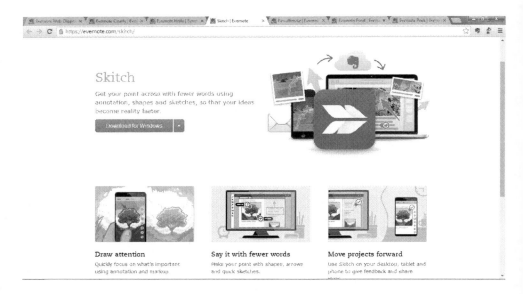

Skitch is a standalone software for annotating pictures. It is a convenient tool that helps you screenshot your notes just with the click of a single button. You get a similar tool within Evernote but if you want to annotate pictures from outside of Evernote you can download Skitch. It works exactly like the annotation tool in Evernote and you can even link your Evernote account to it so when you annotate a picture in Skitch you can then save it to Evernote.

Here is a step-by-step guide for you to follow: First, to screenshot your file, use the "Skitch" editor. It can help you screenshot just about anything including webpages, pictures, notes, reminders, files, pages etc.

Once you screenshot it, it will appear under the heading "screen snap" and you can use your various annotating options such as the arrows, the writing feature, the enhancing feature etc.

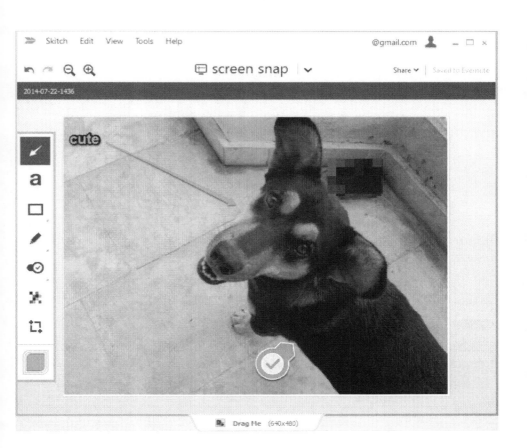

Penultimate

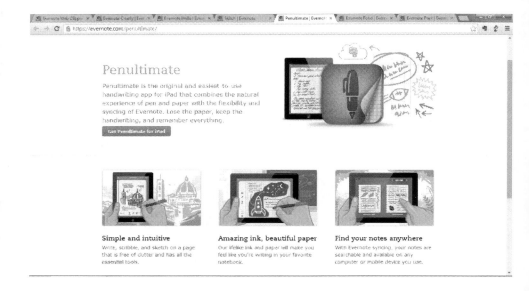

Penultimate is a handwriting app for the iPad. It is considered to be the best app for handwriting and offers a reasonable experience of writing with real ink on real paper. It comes with the ability to link your Evernote account to the app so you can save your handwritten notes on Evernote with the click of a button.

Evernote Food

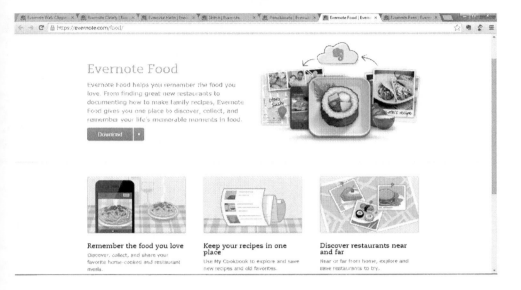

Evernote Food is an app for those who love their food. It can help you store recipes, take pictures and make notes of your favorite meals. It can also help you discover great restaurants near your location. This feature is especially useful for bachelors and housewives alike. The former can look for hotels to eat at and the latter can capture their various recipes and also attach pictures of the same. It is also a good tool for you to start blogging about food or come up with your own recipe book. All you have to do is list out recipes and attach pictures and compile all of them, your easy cookbook is now ready. You can use it for all types of recipes and can have a separate section for each. So you can have entrees, starters, desserts etc. and easily record information in it.

Evernote Peek

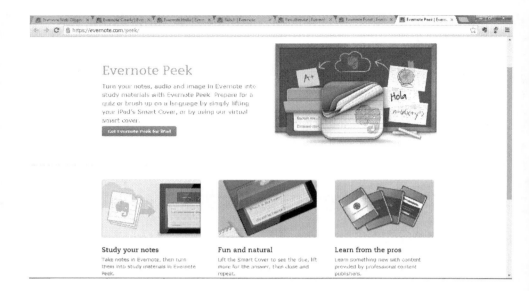

Evernote Peek is for students who need to study their notes. It turns all of your notes, whether they are text, audio, pictures or video, into study notes and quizzes. This is an app only for the iPad and you can use the smart cover to peek at the question. If you lift the cover further you can get the answer. If you don't have a smart cover you can use the virtual smart cover to peek at the quiz. You can also get study material from professional content publishers.

These 7 apps and plug-ins can help you make Evernote the center of your work, studies and life. There are also a lot of developers making add-ons and apps that work well with Evernote. Since there are so many apps that offer different functionality, it's beyond the scope of this book but you can find apps best suited to your personal requirements by a quick search online.

PART TWO

- Evernote Advanced -

Chapter 4: Get the Most Out of Evernote

B y now you've learned all the basics of Evernote. Even with this basic knowledge, I'm sure you can see how beneficial Evernote can be in your life. But to get the most out of Evernote you need to learn some advances tips and tricks that we'll talk about now.

Keyboard Shortcuts

When you use software a lot, it makes sense to learn its keyboard shortcuts. It might seem that shortcuts only save a few milliseconds but when you add them up throughout the day, day in day out, it adds up to a lot. Besides, if you can use Evernote fluidly, it will change the way you experience it. So here are some of the most common shortcuts for the Evernote desktop application:

Action	Shortcut	
	Windows	Mac
New Note	Ctrl + N	Cmd + N
New Notebook	Ctrl + Shift + N	Shift + Cmd + N
New Tag	Ctrl + Shift + T	Ctrl + Cmd + N
Search	F6	Alt + Cmd + F
Minimize Window	Alt + F4	Cmd + M
Quit	Ctrl + Q	Cmd + Q

Show/Hide Sidebar	F10	Alt + Cmd + S
Add Hyperlink	Ctrl + K	Cmd + K
Rename Selected Note	F2	Cmd + L
Remove Formatting	Ctrl + Space	Shift + Cmd + F

For a more detailed shortcut list visit MakeUseOf.com where you can download shortcut cheat sheets for Evernote for both Windows and Mac.

Tags

Evernote users are highly polarized on the topic of tags. Some think that tags are completely useless and only lead to clutter, while others think that tags are the best way of organizing your notes and notebooks are meaningless. Every user comes somewhere between these two opposing views. The truth is that both notebooks and tags can be used alone to organize your notes.

However, the most benefit is to be achieved by combining both notebooks and tags. Notebooks are similar to a filing cabinet. You have notebook stacks that are like drawers in a filing cabinet and the notebooks inside each stack are like the folders inside the drawers. Your notes go inside one or the other folder inside one or the other drawer.

Tags, on the other hand, are like a cross referencing system. You can tag notes inside different folders and drawers, using the same tag, and when you open that tag, you can view all the notes in one place, even if they are in completely different notebook stacks. You can also add multiple tags to every note, which means that you are making the single note accessible from different areas.

For example if you have a receipt that you want to save for tax purposes, you can add it to a notebook named tax inside a stack named finances. You can also add tags to that note such as receipt, exemptible, expenditure etc. So while there is only one note that resides in only one location, you can also access it using any of the tags.

If at first all this sounds confusing, don't worry because every Evernote user has felt that way; hence the extreme opinions about tags. But as you use Evernote more and more, you will get a hang of using tags. In the last part, we'll talk in more detail about how to organize your life using notebooks, stacks and tags.

Meanwhile, a few tips to remember while using tags are:

- Limit the number of tags you create as they can easily get out of hand.

- Have a proper system of naming tags, so that you don't end up forgetting what tag you gave to a similar item in the past.

- You can use a symbol in front of certain tags such as first names. For example if you use ^ before all first names like ^John, ^Mike etc. then when you want to tag a note with a first name all you need to do is type the ^ symbol and a list of all the names will drop down and you can choose the appropriate name from there.

- You can nest tags within tag collections for better organization. Unlike notebook stacks, which can only be one level deep, tag collections can go as deep as you want. To nest tags just drag and drop the child tag on to the parent tag and it will become a tag collection.

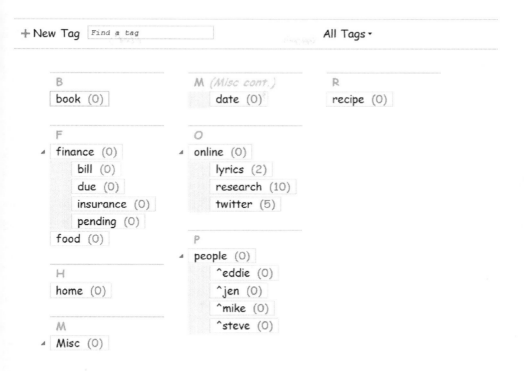

Advanced Searching

When you start creating a lot of notes, you will truly begin to witness the usefulness of Evernote but it will also get harder to find your notes. In the beginning you can simply scan through the list of your notebooks to find the right note but after a while it will become important to learn some advanced searching tricks to help you quickly find what you are looking for.

You need to learn a few search operators. Using "intitle:" before your search term will search for the word in only the titles of notes. So if you search for "intitle: meeting" it will search for all the notes that have the word meeting in the title.

Use "notebook:notebook-name" to search for notes only in that particular notebook. "tag: family" will only search for notes that have been tagged with "family".

When you type multiple words in the search box, such as "tax receipts 2014", Evernote will search for notes that contain all the three terms. Instead if you want to search for any of the search terms you can use the "any:" operator. For example, "any: red apple fruit" will search for notes that contain any of the three words.

For a complete list of operators read this <u>Evernote knowledge base article</u>. Some of these operators may seem confusing at first but once you start using them, you'll memorize them and it will become very easy to search Evernote.

Another tip to remember is that you can save your searches for later use. So if you create an advanced search that you might like to use in the future you can easily save it. In the last part I'll talk about how you can create certain advanced searches and save them for repeated use to increase your productivity.

Apart from searching for your file, the app also gives you the option of searching for data and information on the internet. How many times have you opened an app and simultaneously wished to search the internet for information? In such a case, you will be forced to either minimize the app or end it all together.

But with the Evernote app, you can access the internet from anytime and anywhere.

You can open Google search just with just the one click and look for absolutely anything under the sun. What's more is that, you do not have to minimize or log out of the app, thereby saving you lots of time and effort.

And you need not do any of your research work prior to opening the app. It will allow you to save data as and when you like, directly from the internet.

Apart from doing full-fledged researches, you can also look up little details such as spellings and grammar and ensure that you have an absolutely flawless file or presentation.

Other data such as videos and images can be clipped and added to notes and you do not have to save them and copy them, paste them etc.

Encryption

Encryption is an option that you can use to hide certain text in your notes. You can select any piece of text and encrypt is from the Format menu. You have to set a passphrase for the encryption. Once you encrypt a piece of text it will appear as a locked encryption icon. It will then ask you to add a passphrase like a pass code to lock the message.

To decrypt the password, you have to select the word or sentence and choose the decrypt option and type in the passphrase that will help you unlock it.

The main function of this feature is to safeguard all your files and data. The feature will help you safeguard all your important data in a very efficient manner.

This option can come in handy while sharing notebooks that contain sensitive data you don't want to share with everyone. If multiple people use the computer at home, this option can help you maintain your privacy.

The feature is also important in order to safeguard your passwords, credit card numbers, pin numbers etc. as they can be stolen or can get lost.

But one thing to be cautious about is that, this passphrase will not be saved by Evernote and you have to be careful with it. There will not be a copy available with Evernote and you have to either memorize it or have it written down for easy reference.

And to make it easier for you to remember it in case you do forget it, then you will be asked to type in a clue like a description of the passphrase. But you have to be careful with the question and type in a cryptic one, as it will be available for anyone to see. You have to keep it vague and avoid direct answers.

The same applies to the passphrase, as you have to keep it rare and vague and something that is not too obvious like your name or last name or date of birth etc.

This feature is especially useful to set test papers, as you can write down the answer to the questions and encrypt it.

The Benefits of Importing Email

As we now know, the Evernote app is incredibly useful to all those that are interested in maximizing their productivity and increasing their work output. We have thus far looked at how you can use the Evernote app to make lists, annotate pictures, edit with ease, use the different widgets etc. Now, we will read in detail on how you can use the Evernote app to import emails and use it to your advantage.

Yes that's right. You can import your emails and work on them in the Evernote. Wouldn't it be simply amazing for you to access all your mails from your app? Imagine the possibilities! You will have the chance to do just so much in a day and increase your overall work potential. Why just work? It will add to your personal and social life as well and you can improve your overall living.

In this segment, we will look at how you can use this app feature to your advantage and make use of it to improve your productivity.

Collecting emails

The main advantage of linking your email to your Evernote is the collection of all the important emails in one place. When you link your emails to your Evernote, you have a chance at collecting everything that is important to you in one place. This means that you have a chance at bookmarking everything that is important and placing them in an accessible place in your device. This safe place being your Evernote notebooks. You can access the mails at any time and from anywhere regardless of whether there is internet or not. As soon as you link the email it will turn into a notebook and get stored in your Evernote.

Ease of use

It is extremely easy to use this feature. Anybody who is new to it can easily adopt as well as those who have used the app for some time. All you have to do is link your email to your notebook. To do so, you must find out what your ever note email address is. Once you find out, you send your mail to that address and find the mail there. It is as simple as that. To find your ever note email address go to settings –> Accounts info -> ever note email to find yours. You can add it to your email contact list.

Reminders

It is now extremely easy for you to have reminders regarding important emails. How many times have you missed something important just because you haven't remembered it? Would it be great if you had a reminder for all your invites instead of it simply sitting in your inbox? Well, with the email to ever note feature, you can now place easy reminders. Say for example you have received a business invitation from your colleague. You forward that to your ever note app and it will automatically get stored as "meeting invitation" notebook along with a reminder stating the date. That way, you will never fall behind on your schedules and keep all your dates.

Automatic

There is an automatic feature which will automatically redirect mails to your Evernote app. You don't have to do it manually and it will automatically go into your inbox. This feature is discussed in detail in the next segment of this book.

De-cluttering

It is now easy to achieve a zero inbox, as you will have a chance to sort everything automatically. You can do away with having to select hundreds of mails and marking them as read. All you have to do is go through all your emails and redirect them into the appropriate notebooks. This will help you keep everything sorted and don't have to open each to know what lies in it. You will not have the problem of personally putting each in a different and appropriate folder and it will automatically get redirected into the rightful folders, given you have added the contacts to the notebook tags.

Bills/ payments

It is now easy for you to track all your bill payments and receipts by linking your email to Evernote. Forward them to your ever note and find them there. Right from your electricity to telephone to credit card bills and online purchases to store purchase, you can find everything in your ever note just by forwarding it. You don't have to worry about losing them or accidentally deleting them. A copy will always be present in your ever note and by tagging them you can have all of them in one place. You will never lose your important bills and receipts ever again!

Tracking

I'm sure you are the type that keeps checking the status of something that you have ordered online to make sure that it is on schedule. If you place many online orders then the ever note app will help you keep track of all of them. Simply forward all the tracking links to your ever note and click on them whenever to track them with ease. You don't have to keep typing in the order number or air way bill number, all you have to do is forward the tracking link to your mail and have it ready to track your order. You can also mark the ones you wish to return and be done with it within a few minutes.

Trip details

Travelling will now be a breeze thanks to the email to Evernote feature. Whether you are planning to take a family holiday or going for a business meeting, all your trip details can now be safely stored in your ever note app. All you have to do is forward your trip details including your airplane ticket, hotel details, transport details etc. and send it to your ever note app. Your app will maintain a record of it for you and you can access it at any time and from anywhere. You can also store your family members' detail in your notebook as a backup.

Newsletter/ data mails

How many times have you read half a newsletter and then forgotten about it thanks to it getting lost in our mail box? Now that problem can be solved for good! All you have to do is create a newsletter notebook and direct all your newsletters there. You will have a chance to accumulate all your newsletters in one place and can read them at anytime and anywhere. You can do the same with lengthy mails that contain important information.

How to automate your Email Delivery

In the previous chapter, we looked at how you can use the email to Evernote feature to optimize your productivity. Now, let us look at how you can automatically redirect these mails into a specific notebook, create tags for it and also set reminders for your emails.

Notebooks

As we know, a notebook contains many notes which all have a similar subject. Your individual notebooks contain notes that are related and have similar data. Similarly, you will have a lot of emails that all have a similar subject. You will want all of them to be filed in the same place. This will minimize your time in looking for a specific notebook and can access it at a faster pace.

So, if you have a specific set of mails that need to be redirected into specific notebooks then here are some things that you can do for them to all land in the same notebook.

Default notebook

If you wish for all your mails to go into a default notebook then you can create a notebook called "all mail" or something similar to store all your emails. This will ensure that you have all your mails in the same notebook. Now to redirect all your mail to this notebook, all you have to do is add in the subject line of your forwarded email @notebook. This will redirect it into the default notebook that you have. This is mainly for those who do not wish to bifurcate their mails and preserve just one notebook for it. But for those that require separate folders for each of their mails can look at the next option.

Specific notebook

Specific notebooks are for those who wish to bifurcate their mails and send them to particular notebooks. Say for example you wish to send all your travel related mails to your travel notebook then all you have to do is add in "@travel" in the subject line and all your travel mail will go there. Similarly, you can have one for work, one for recipes, one for leisure etc. you can create as many notebooks as you like and redirect all related mail there. This will ensure that you know exactly where to find what you are looking for.

Tags

As we know, tags are a big part of ever note. Tags are important as you can easily navigate to where the tag is placed in the notebook in order to access the thing you are looking for. So if you wish to tag your emails in your notebooks then here is what you can do for it.

When you wish to tag a mail then simply include a # followed by the name of the tag. This will ensure that the tag is specifically redirected into the right place. So say for example you wish to send a recipe to your recipe notebook. You can send @recipes #cheesecakes. This will ensure that the tag "cheesecakes" is added to the note. When you search for cheesecakes then this recipe will show up. Similarly, you can tag as many things as you like but make sure that each one is preceded by the # symbol otherwise it will not get tagged.

Reminders

Reminders are for those that wish to have a reminder for an important event show up on their ever note. This is especially important for all those people that have difficulties in remembering something important. Say for example you have a problem remembering to attend an important meeting. All you have to do is place a reminder tag and remember the event with ease.

Here is how you can make use of this feature.

Just add an exclamatory symbol before the date or the day or time of the event and your app will send you a reminder. For example: you wish to remember Monday then all you have to do is add "!Monday" in your subject line and you will receive a reminder for it. Similarly, you can add "!23/7/2015" and you will have a reminder on that day. You can send as many reminders as you like and as much into the future as you prefer. Apart from just adding in the date or the day you can also add in "tomorrow" or "today" as that will also allow you to receive your due reminders.

So a typical subject line incorporating all these elements will look like this.
Subject: Title of notebook !reminder details @notebook name #tag
Birthday party !30/5/2015 @parties #John
So this is a birthday party for John reminder on the 30 of this month.

Similarly, you can automatically redirect all your mails to the right notebooks.

Remember that all these need to be put in the subject line and not in the body of the mail.

You can also automatically redirect mails from certain senders by making use of the automatic mail filters. Say for example you want all of John's emails to go into your work notebook, you simply instruct your mail to redirect it to the work notebook and the email address your ever note email address.

You can also add in something to an existing note in a notebook. All you have to do is add a "+" sign in the subject line and the body of the mail will be appended to the note you have specified in the subject line.

There are many other software available on the Internet which will help in automatically redirect certain mails that you have labeled in your Gmail. You can look up the best and download it to help you reduce the effort put in forwarding mails to your ever note app.

There is a small difference between the free version and the premium version in that, the former will have a limit of 50 emails per day and the latter has a limit of 250 emails per day. So you can buy the premium version if you have a lot of emails to sort through in a day.

Scan Documents Using CamScanner

We looked at the benefits of having the email to ever note feature and now, let us shift focus to the scanning feature.

We have already seen that you can screenshot anything that you like and annotate over it in the ever note app. This will help you during your presentations and many other such works. But what you screen shot is already present in your phone or something that is accessible on it. Say for example you screen shot a picture from the internet and worked on it or imported an email and annotate. But what happens if what you need is not available on your device? What if there is no soft copy of it and you only have the hard copy with you? Well, you use the CamScanner app.

The cam scanner app is one that allows you to digitize all your hard copies. Doesn't that sound absolutely wonderful? Forget having to carry around bulky scanners to scan your documents, all you need is the app installed on your phone or tablet that will take a picture of the document and voila! Your scanned document is ready.

Here is what you can do with the CamScanner

Convert all your hardcopy text and graphic documents into soft copy just by clicking a picture of it. Place the paper or document in a well-lit place and click the picture. It will not take any more than a few seconds for this to happen.

It is possible for you to do a panoramic shot and place two or three documents next to each other and you can have several documents all scanned in one go. This will help you in having all the information in a single page.

The app is designed to crop the documents and make it as clear as possible for you to read. It also adjusts the contrast and other quality related features in order to help you see the text and graphic clearly. This is known as the smart enhance feature. Apart from the automatic changes you can also choose from preset modes that will help you personalize the documents.

You can easily prepare PDF files for your scanned documents and use it to append into your notebooks. Apart from just papers and sheets you can also scan whiteboards, bills, receipts etc.

Once you are done digitizing the documents you can export it to the ever note app. In fact, you can save the scanned copies to ever note app and work on them with the tools provided by the app. You can crop it, annotate and do what you wish to with the scanned copy.

You can also collaborate and share the scanned copy. You can email the PDF or the JPG files to your collaborators and they can work on it and send it back to you with equal ease.

There is also cloud storage facility that will help you maintain a copy of it on all your devices.

There is a choice between the free version and the premium paid version. The free version is available for free across all platforms including android, iOS and windows. All you have to do is look for the CamScanner and download it. You can use this to test the app and understand what features it provides and then go for the premium version which comes at a price of $4.99 a month and $49.99 a year.

The free version offers you 200 MB of cloud space and you can collaborate with a maximum of 10 people at one time. You will also have an easy search option that will allow you to quickly search for something from your documents. You can also synchronize everything across all your devices and this is a primary feature on the free version. You also get the feature of water marking over the documents, which is a part of the free version.

The premium version provides a whole host of other features that are beneficial for you. This includes a cloud space of 10 G, creating a collage of several pages together, automatically uploading to ever note app, sending the documents after password protecting it, adding an expiry date to the password, synchronizing all the documents across all your devices, customizing the watermarks on your documents and collaborating with 50 people (per document) at once.

It is up to you to decide on whether you want the free version or the premium version.

How to use Web Clipper and how to Bookmark Important Sites

When it comes to the ever note app, everything is so easy and well thought for that you will have absolutely no difficulty in using it. All you have to do is think of it and it will be readily available for you to use. There are so many small things that people still find interesting such as the web clipper facility.

This feature was mentioned earlier and gave you a gist of what the web clipper feature is all about. Now, we will look at it in detail to help you understand each and every aspect of it.

As you know, the web clipper is meant to help you clip a webpage or a part of it and store it in your ever note app. You can then do what you like with it including reading, editing, annotating and sharing.

Ever note updated the feature in August 2014 and the newer version is extremely useful and much better than the previous one.

To start using this feature, download the web clipper from the store. You will see that the ever note elephant button appears on your browser tool bar once download is complete. If it is not visible then you must expand your tool bar to see it.

Once you have it ready, go to the page where you wish to clip. Click on the elephant button and choose the type of clip you wish to have, viz. article clip, full-page clip, screenshot clip, bookmark clip or URL clip.

When you choose the article clip, the app will automatically choose the main body of the article and clip it for you. This will save you the effort of zooming into something to clip it. However, if you are not satisfied with the clip then you can simply zoom in or zoom out using the "+" or "-" buttons and then clip the part that you like.

If you choose the simplified article option then the app with zoom in to only the article and clear away everything else that will distract you while reading. This will help you concentrate only on the article and you can finish reading it fast.

If you choose the full-page option then the entire page will be clipped including all the headers and footers and everything that is present on the page. You will get everything that the page is displaying without any deductions. This is best if you wish to work on different parts of the page individually.

The web clipper bookmark feature is a new addition and a unique concept. If you don't have enough space or don't wish to clutter your notebooks then you can simply clip the URL of the page or just an image or a few lines that will help you return to the page with ease. All you have to do is paste the URL or reverse search the image and you will get what you are looking for in a matter of seconds.

If you choose the screenshot option, you can choose a certain part of it and crop the image from it to use and modify.

You can also save a PDF document and attach it to a new note in your ever note app.

Apart from websites, you can also clip from your email. You can clip a part of a mail or an entire mail from your Gmail account and use in your ever note app. Similarly, you can also clip from outlook and use in your Evernote app.

Once you are done with all your clippings you can neatly organize them in the app. You can add in tags and organize everything neatly and in an orderly fashion.

Next, you can annotate over these clippings. This means that you can write, draw, highlight over them. You can use any of the standard annotation tools for this including choosing from the shapes, the color change options, the crop, the pen tool, the pixelator tool the zoom in and zoom out tool etc. you can do what you like on the clipped image and can also mix two and come up with a hybrid image. It is completely up to you and you can save multiple copies of your annotated images with each one having a different annotation.

It is extremely easy for you to share these clips with others. It is obvious that you will want to share the modified web clips with others and for this, all you have to do is copy your clip's URL and paste it into a chat session with a friend or message it or WhatsApp etc. it is as simple as that. But if you want a more formal approach then you can mail it to a friend or a colleague. Simply clip it and copy the url and paste in the email subject line or body and send.

It is extremely easy to search for a web clip as ever note not only makes all your typed or hand written text available for search but also the text that is present within a cropped image. So if you tag some words from it then it will be very easy for you to search for it and even if you have not tagged it then typing in the most prominent word from the clip will put forth the clipped image. It is really easy to look for anything and everything once you save it to the ever note app.

The ever note app is smart enough to link two or more articles or images that you have clipped from the same page or site. It will automatically link them and you can search in related results and find that the app displays all of them together. It will batch all the related articles in one place so that you can access them with ease.

Another great feature of the web clipper is that, it is possible for you to customize the clipper. That is, you can choose a default action to clip like a page or a URL or you can choose to link all the related results etc. it is possible for you to customize the web clipper feature to any extent you like.

The new version offers you the Reminders feature. You can click on the clock button to place a reminder on a clip. This will enable you to remember something like share the clip or do something with it. If you have clipped a date and a venue for something then this feature will help you remember to make it to that place. So this is the other unique clipper feature that makes the web clipper a winner.

Email to Evernote

To send an email from any email service provider such as Gmail, yahoo etc. to your Evernote account, you just need to forward it to the email id provided to you by Evernote. You can find this email id in Tools>>Account Info.

The subject of your forwarded email will control how and where the note is created. The structure you need to follow is:

Email Subject = [Title of note] ![Optional date for reminder] @[Notebook] #[Tag]

For example if you forward an email from your friend Paul with the subject: "Party Invitation !2014/12/24 @personal #invitation #^Paul", then a note with the title "Party Invitation" will be created in the notebook "personal". Tags of "invitation" and "^Paul" will be added to the note and a reminder will be set for 24th December 2014.

This is a powerful way of collecting important emails in one place. This ability of using Evernote without actually opening Evernote is what sets it apart.

IFTTT Automation

Another way of using Evernote from outside is by using the website www.ifttt.com. It stands for IF This Then That. This is a really powerful website that helps you automate your online tasks. You can sign up for free and start building your automation "recipes".

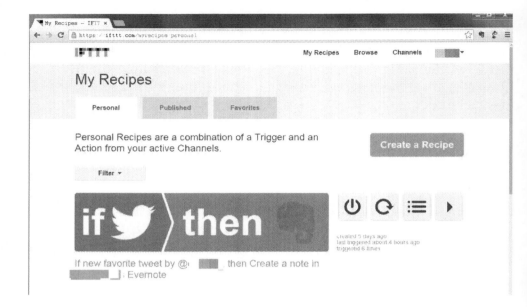

To build a recipe you need to define what "this" and "that" will be in the equation. For example you can create a recipe to create a note every time you favorite a tweet. To do this you'll first need to select your twitter account and set the action of favorite a tweet as "this". Then connect your Evernote account and select the notebook you want the notes to be saved in. So you can create a notebook called "twitter" or "inspiration" and set up an automation so that every time you find an interesting or inspiration tweet and you favorite it, it automatically gets saved in your Evernote account as a note.

There are hundreds of recipes that you can create this way and if you find this task daunting, just search through preexisting recipes on the IFTTT website. Chances are that everything you want to do already has a recipe created for it.

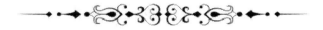

PART THREE

- Evernote Expert -

Chapter 5: Life Management Using Evernote

Here's how Evernote users are divided into three groups:

1. Those who hear about Evernote and try it out for a while and then stop using it. They learn the basics of Evernote that we talked about in the first part of this book but after using it for a month or two, they can't understand what everyone is raving about and give up.

2. Those who learn the advanced tricks of Evernote and use it for many months or even years. They can understand how powerful Evernote is but after a while they get stuck and it's too much work to collect everything and eventually they limit the use of Evernote for one or two tasks such as curating reading material from the internet.

3. And then there are those who learn to creatively use Evernote to manage their whole life. These are people who rave about Evernote and get on the nerves of everyone else.

The reason why not everyone can use Evernote to its highest potential is ironically the same reason why Evernote is so powerful. And that reason is that Evernote doesn't tell you how to manage your life. It is just a tool and doesn't pretend to be a manager. But because it sticks to what it knows best, the creative person can really utilize the full potential of this powerful tool.

In this last part, we'll talk about how you too can use Evernote to manage your life. Since every person is different, has a unique life and a distinctive outlook towards life management, there is no one-size-fits-all system that will work for everyone. So I'll not try to tell you how you should manage your life. Instead I'll try to emulate Evernote and provide you with creative ideas that you can use or ignore as you see fit.

Ubiquitous Capture

Think of Evernote as an extension of your brain combined with an outsourced office. To make full use of it, you need to first learn to capture any and all information of your life and store it in Evernote. Here's a list of things you can do:

- All work related documents go into Evernote. Digital documents such as emails are easy to import. Hardcopy documents should also be scanned and saved in Evernote, which makes the information easier to store, handle and retrieve. You can do away with all unnecessary papers and simply use the ever note as your go to device to look at all your papers at once.

- All bills, receipts, forms, contracts, highlighted passages from your favorite books, should all be scanned into Evernote.

- All your life goals, dreams, ambitions, plans etc. should be stored in Evernote.

- Use Evernote as your address book and store all information regarding people on Evernote.

- Use Evernote to write your daily journal. Evernote works even better than dedicated journaling apps because you can use any of your devices to write in the same journal. You can scan entries written on paper. And you can search all your journal entries easily. You can also add pictures and other documents to your journal.

- All your online reading can also be stored in Evernote and you can read it offline.

- You can send inspirational quotes, pictures etc. from the internet into Evernote as well.

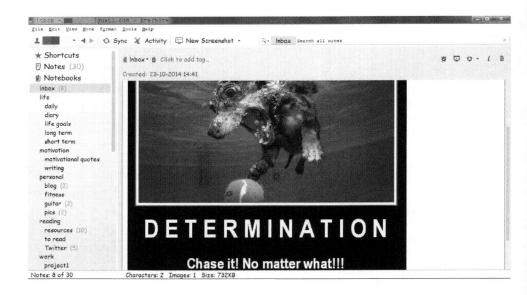

Organizing the Information

Once you begin capturing information from all spheres of your life and importing it to Evernote, the next step is to organize the information in a logical way. This method of course will depend on what suits you best. As mentioned earlier some people use only tags and others use only notebooks. I recommend using both.

Start by creating notebook stacks for the major areas of your life. An example is to have stacks named:

- **Work:** This stack will contain notebooks related to different areas of your work. You can also create sub categories here that will tell you what the work relates to. It can be in regard to projects or people that you work with.

- **Personal:** This stack will contain notebooks related to personal life. You will need to keep this organized as well in order to lead a productive life. Wasting your time is never an option and the more organized that you remain the better your life will be.

- **Life:** This stack will contain notebooks for your life goals, yearly goals, plans, diary etc. Everybody has to have one and without it, you will only get lost. So don't waste any time and start preparing your lists and goals at the earliest.

- **Reading:** This stack will contain reading material that you capture online or eBooks that you have to read. This is for all those that like to read a lot and is sure to help in having everything you need well organized.

- **Motivation:** This stack will contain notebooks that contain inspirational stuff. Everybody needs to be motivated and so, if you have a stack of notes that will inspire you to aim higher and achieve bigger things in life then nothing like it.

Remember that notebooks can only go one level deep. So while everything can be covered under work and personal, we can't create multiple level stacks within these two stacks.

Also create a separate notebook called !nbox which is outside all stacks. Make this your default notebook. Notice the "!" in place of the "i". Use this to keep the inbox notebook right at top of the sidebar. Whenever you are not sure about which notebook a note goes in, just send it to !nbox and sort it out later.

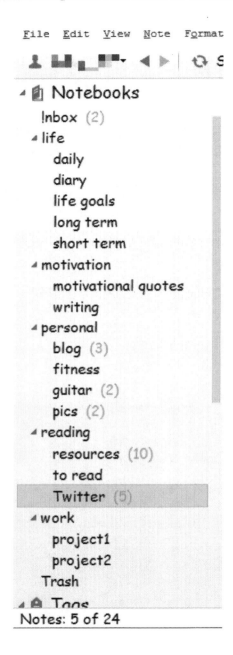

Don't over think this and just create a few basic notebooks for now. As you use Evernote more and more, you'll realize that you don't use certain notebooks or that you need a new notebook or that two notebooks can be merged. This is a work in progress and will get better as you use it.

You shouldn't have more than 10-15 notebooks as it can get confusing. Evernote allows you to have up to 250 notebooks and many people try to use them all, but it is better to have a few basic notebooks to separate the major areas of life and then use tags for more detailed sorting. Evernote allows you to use 100,000 tags but again, the lesser you have the better it will be.

The most important thing to remember while tagging is to use a constant nomenclature for your tags. Tags are case sensitive and singular and plural tags are considered different tags. If you don't have a system for naming your tags you can soon complicate the system by having too many tags. The best practice is to use lowercase characters and singular words all the time.

An example of using tags with notebooks together:

Say you have a notebook in your work stack called meetings. Within that notebook you store all notes related to your work meetings. These can be meeting notes, presentations and schedule for your future meetings and appointments. You can tag the notes that are just for scheduling meetings with the tag "appointment".

So when you just want to look at the notes that contain scheduling information instead of going to the meetings notebook you can just go to the appointment tag. Also if you set a personal appointment with a doctor and save it in a notebook in the personal stack you can still access it with the appointment tag if you have tagged it correctly.

As you can see the meeting notebook lets you see all your meeting related notes in one place while the appointment tag lets you see all your appointments in one place. When to make a notebook and when to make a tag will depend on how you look at your life. As you use Evernote more and more you'll find that certain terms work better as tags while others as notebooks.

The Life Stack

Make a stack called life and inside create all or some of these notebooks:

- **Long Term:** This should contain notes such as your life purpose or mission statement, life goals, and value list etc. You will use these notes for reference and update them throughout your life. You will never delete what is here unless it is really eating away into your space.

- **Short Term:** This notebook should contain several notes such as a yearly goals checklist, timetable, yearly review checklist, review reports etc. You can tag each note with the year and month it belongs to so you can separate the old information. Although it is tough to put it into a time frame, something like 1 year or 6 months is a good time frame to operate within.

- **Diary:** This notebook will contain notes that will form your daily journal. If you write multiple times in a day, create subheadings within the note and keep one note per day for easier organization.

- **Daily:** This notebook will contain notes that you use for your day to day time management. It will contain your daily task list that can be a checklist where you check off each item as and when you finish doing it. At the end of the day you can check the notes in this notebook to see how you did.

- **Someday Maybe:** This is a notebook for those dreams of yours that seem impossible right now. Check it frequently and move dreams out of it and into the short-term goals list.

◢ life
   daily
   diary
   life goals
   long term
   short term

Use the life stack as your main life planning area. These notebooks are just an example for you to build upon. In the end how you manage your life will depend completely on you.

Saved Searches

You can save a lot of time by creating few saved searches that you use frequently. Here are a few examples:

- "created:day" will show all the notes you made today. You can save it as "today". For yesterday use, "created:day-1 - created:day". For the notes created in the last month use "created:day-30"; this will show all the notes created in the last 30 days.

- "resource:image/*" will show all the notes that contain images. You can also use this for other resource types such as audio, documents etc.

- "source:mobile.*" will show all the notes created from your mobile.

- "source:email.smtp" will show all the notes you send from your email.

- "source:web.clip" will show notes you clipped using the web clipper extension of Evernote.

- "todo:false" will show all the checklists you have which have at least one unchecked box. This can come in handy while searching for things on different checklists that you still have to do. "todo:true" will show checklists that have at least one checked box. "todo:*" will show all the checklists whether or not they've been checked.

- "encryption:" will show all notes that have something encrypted.

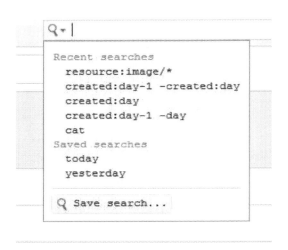

Basics Steps of Getting Things Done

The getting things done is a concept introduced by David Allen, who explained in detail how people can get things done with ease and in little time. Getting things done is a good concept to adopt and used with your eve note app, you have a chance to increase your productivity and get things done faster. Remember that being organized always helps in doing things at a faster pace and that is what the concept of GTD relies on. You have the chance to finish your tasks faster and attain faster and better results every time. You must try and use this concept with your ever note app and get done with your tasks at the earliest.

Here are the different steps of GTD explained and are meant to educate you on the topic in a better way.

Capture

The very step is to capture everything that is in your head. That is all your to do lists, everything you wish to finish, everything that needs immediate attention, things that are not important etc. Make sure you record everything in your notes. The main aim is to have everything handy and ready. Don't worry if you are choosing to record it in a rough way. You can take it down in your note pad or just some place as long as you are taking it out of your head and putting it on paper. Remember that it should be a combination of things that you have always wanted to do for a long time and also things that crop up in your mind at the moment when you prepare the list. Try and make the list as conclusive as possible and induce all your ideas and thoughts. Remember that you are trying to get every thought you have on paper so that you don't forget about it after a while. Don't hesitate to put ideas and to dos related to your work, home and other such aspects of your life. Some people prefer to first write it down on a piece of paper and then transfer it to their digital diary or scan the sheet of paper.

Clarify

The second step is known as clarify. As the name suggests, this is the stage where you clarify everything that you have written down. You have to go through it in detail and see whether what you have written down is doable or impossible. Say for example, you wrote "bake 200 cakes for charity" if this is not actionable immediately then file it for a later date. You must preferably write down the date when you would like to carry out the activity. This can be a near date or a future date. If there is something that is impossible to carry out then simply mark it for reference. The idea is to not discard anything and hold on to everything. So try and keep everything that you have written down. Now look at the ones that are actionable. There will be those that need immediate attention and those that can wait a little but everything needs to be completed necessarily. You will have to go through everything that you have listed one by one and make sure that you deal with them as and when possible.

Organize

The next step is to organize everything that you have. That is, organize everything in such ways that you know exactly which ones need to be given priority and which ones can wait. Organize them into individual categories and file them as per their priorities. Say for example you have "work on project" and "finish gardening". You will have to prioritize work on project and so, you must place it on top of the priority list. This will ensure that you do the important task first and then move to the next one. Remember that this is still in the planning stage and you are not required to leap into action right away. Just make sure that you redirect all the tasks into the right categories based on priority and urgency. You can put it into the different categories and name them whatever you think is befitting. You must have easy access to your lists and also have the function of ticking them off once they are completed. This applies to both the entire lists and the individual items mentioned in it. Once you have successfully completed this task, you can move on to the next step of the getting things done process.

Reflect

Reflect refers to looking at your lists and updating them from time to time. You can also look at them to determine whether what you have recorded is appropriate. This means that you check if it is possible for you to execute the tasks that you have listed down. You must assess whether they are really doable and if it is possible for you to finish them within the assigned time frame. This step is important, as you must follow up on everything that you do. You cannot simply make lists and forget about it. That's like making a cake batter, sticking it in the oven and forgetting about it. If you decide to make a list then you must stick with it and also refer to it from time to time to make sure that you are doing everything correctly. You can refer to it once a week, preferably at the beginning of the week, and assess where you stand. If you have finished something then tick it off, if something is left to be done then prioritize it. You need to assign yourself a particular time to assess your lists on a weekly basis and make sure that you review your list at the same time every week in order to fall into a regular habit.

Engage

The last step of course is to engage in the activity. This is where the action begins. You have to start performing your tasks. Your to do's are to be executed now and you must look at the things that are doable at the earliest and in the most resourceful manner. This means that you start by choosing the most important thing on your priority list and go about it. Your list would have listed what you need to do and when it needs to be done so, you must go about it accordingly. Remember that you must start performing the tasks in such a way that you get done with it at the earliest. However, don't rush it. Dedicate enough time to it in order to execute it in the best possible way. Once you are done with it, you must run to the list and tick it off. Make sure you are not spending too much time doing something that can be done at a faster pace or something once done cannot be bettered. Learn to move to the next task as soon as possible without pondering over something for a long time.

Basic Requirements to GTD with Evernote

In the previous chapter, we looked at the concept of getting things done in detail and now, we will look at what you need to do to make it work worth the ever note app.

As was said before, the two will work great together and you will have a chance to do more in a short time. Here, we will look at the things you need to gtd with ever note.

Ever note

This is the first thing that you will need when you wish to gtd with ever note. You will have to download it and create an account. You will then have to login in order to gtd. The process is fairly simple and you will read about how to gtd with ever note in the next segment of this book. So start with the basics and download the app on your phone, tablet or your pc and get ready to gtd.

Clarity

The next thing to have is clarity. You need to be clear on what needs to be done and when. You will need a list of things to go as per and be done with them after assigning priorities. You will have to understand the concept of gtd as well in order to know exactly what needs to be done to get things done at the earliest. The clearer you are, the better the output.

Knowledge

The next step is to have knowledge on how things work in ever note, I am sure you have a fair idea of what notebooks, notes, tags and reminders are and how they work. But if you do not know it then you need to read on it as soon as possible and familiarize yourself with the concepts in order to work with the ever note and gtd at the earliest. So it is key to know how you can operate the ever note in order to make progress.

Patience

Last but not the least, you need to have patience. If you have no patience then it will be very difficult for you to gtd with ever note. You need to remain as patient as possible and not rush things. Giving is never a choice for you and you need to remain putting and get things do around your house, your work place and in your social life in order to lead a well organized and productive life.
Now that we have looked at all the things you need to do in order to get things done, let us now look at how you can set up a gtd system in your ever note app.

How To Set Up GTD Notebooks

In the previous chapter, we looked at the things you need to incorporate the GTD into your Evernote and now we will look at how you can set up the notebooks to help you with Gtd.

To get started, you have to create a few notebooks; these are explained in detail here.

Basic notebook (inbox)

This is the first thing to start with. You need a basic notebook to start with. You have to have one where everything that is related to GTD can be redirected. You need a stack that can contain all the notebooks that consist of what you need to get done. You can name this notebook whatever you like but GTD collection is a good name for it. You will redirect everything that needs to be sorted as your "capture" here. So it will contain a lot of things at any given point, which will have to be sorted out later.

Default notebook

You have to make this your default notebook. This is important, as you will have to have everything go into the same box every time. For this, you can make the notebook a default notebook. For that, you have to right click on the notebook and go to properties and select the box next to make my default notebook. You can also tick the box when you are creating the notebook in the first place. Everything that you want to go over there will automatically go there. You can email information to this notebook and also send all your lists here.

Gtd notebook/ process notebook

The next notebook to create is the gtd notebook. Here, you can add all the things that need to be done now or those things that are doable. As we saw in the previous chapter, there can be a lot of things that you will want to do but only a few things can actually be done. So those things need to be added in here. You will have to clarify and organize them in order to add the lists and information to this book.

Reference

Your last notebook is your reference notebook. Here, you will add all those things that do not require immediate attention and can be performed later. They can also contain information that you need to carry out a particular task. These three should be your standard go to reference lists when you wish to use gtd coupled with ever note.

Reminders

You can add reminders to all your tasks and make sure that you carry them out on time. You will have reminders that will remind you to get done with something as soon as it is time to start doing it. This is a rather new feature in the ever note gtd.

Lists

You will have to add in a list of things to do so that they are prioritized and you can finish doing them at the earliest. Let us look at some of the most common lists that people prepare for their ever note gtd.

Schedules

People's lives are all about schedules and agendas. You will have to prepare one in order to go as per it and lead a smooth life. You have to schedule everything that you wish to do in a day, in a week, in a month etc. once you have the schedule, you need to follow it accordingly and also use it to sort the material into the three different notebooks that were mentioned before.

Errands

You will have to run a lot of errands around the house and work. This means that you need to run around and do things for your house as also for your work. If you remain disorganized then it won't work for you. So try and remain as organized as possible. Again, list it based on priority and try to keep it as simple as possible in order to have easy reference.

Projects

You will have several projects to complete which can be both work related and house related. You have to list out all your completed and to do projects in order to get done with them at the earliest. You will also have to sort through them and assign them priorities. Follow them as per their priorities and once you are done, get down to engaging in them.

Work

Here, list out everything that needs to be done at work. You will have a million things to do and if you don't list it then you will never get done with it. Once you get the hang of listing things out and following it accordingly, you will realize that your productivity has increased and you are in a position to leave work early. So list out everything and attach a priority to it.

Personal

Just like work related lists, you must prepare personal lists. Here, you will have to add in all those personal things that need to be taken care of at the earliest. This can be related to your family members, your house, your pets etc. everything that needs to be done must be listed out and prioritized for easy operation.

Social

These are for all the things that you wish to do socially. It can be in terms of hanging out with your friends, what you wish to do socially etc. prepare lists here as well and lend them priority.

Calls

You will want to sort through your calls and messages. Once you do, make a list of priorities such as call Adam now or Call Dennis later. Add in reminders for your calls.

Mails

The same extends to emails. Go through them and prioritize what needs to be replied to immediately and what can wait. Remember, there is nothing as being too organized and more is less when it comes to increasing your productivity. So take these lists up seriously and make sure that you follow them through. You can attach reminders here too and do as required; on time.
Don't forget to tag everything as you go.

How To Set Up Tags for GTD

It is obvious that you will have to introduce tags to your GTD notebooks. You know exactly how tags work and why they are useful to your overall ever note experience. Let us now look at the tags that you can add and what each one stands for.

Before we do that, here is how you can set up the tags.

We know that tags are used to separate the notebooks based on their content and urgency. To add tags, start by going to the edit menu and click on tags. Once the box appears, start typing the name of the tags. But this can be slightly tedious if you wish to add in many tags. For that, you can create a note and click on the "click to add tag" option to add in the tags. You can then add in your tags one by one and hit return to go to the next line.

The tags can be anything that helps you know about the note's nature. You need not stick to standard jargons and can add in anything that you think is fitting. Here is looking at some of the most common tags get used and you can choose to add these to your GTD notebooks.

- What

This is the first and most important tag. This is for all the data that describes what the task is all about. You have to know what you are doing before you start doing it and this tag is sure to help you along the way as you will know exactly what needs to be done and the tag will help you find the description of the task.

- .When

This is the tag that tells you when the task needs to be carried out. It is obvious that you need information on when something needs to be done and so, you use this tag to tag all the schedules for your to do lists. This tag is also to tell you when something needs to be done and when you need to move to the next task. Let us look at the sub categories or sub tags for each reference.

- !Daily

This is for all the tasks that need to be carried out on a daily basis. This is probably the most used tag in this category. You will have to tag everything that simply must be finished on a daily basis. This can include checking email, replying to them, calling the boss, picking kids from school, meeting friends etc.

- 1-Now

This is for all tasks that need immediate attention. You need to mention tasks that need to be done immediately and cannot wait any longer. These are for tags such as pick kids right away, take out garbage right now etc. remember to use this tag only for the most important tasks that need to be done.

- 2-Next

This tag is for the tasks that need to be performed next, that is, after finishing the "now" tasks. You must add this tag to all those tasks that need to be compulsorily done as a follow up to the now tasks. Say for example ice the cake after you bake the cake.

- 3-Soon

This tag is for all those things that need to be done soon enough and can be done at any time during the day. So say you have to clean the fans. You can do this in the afternoon or the night but needs to be done within the day.

- 4-Later

This tag is for all those things that can be performed later. So it can be for things that are not urgent to finish. You can do them at any time during the next month or few months and are not necessarily important.

- 5-Someday

This tag is for all those things that need to be done someday. That someday might not be in the near future and can be any day. As long as it will get done, you can simply tag it with this and leave it as it is.

- 6-Waiting

This is for all those tasks whose result you are waiting for. This is because these tasks are someone else's to do and you are waiting for them to be completed by the concerned people. You might have to remind them to do it.

- .Where

This is a tag for all those tasks mentioning where it is to be performed. So this can be in office or at home or at a party or at a meeting etc. basically, this tag is to tell you where a certain task needs to be carried out. Let us look at the sub tags.

- @home

This is for all your home tasks.

- @work

This is for all your work tasks.

- @ life

This is for all things related to your life in general.

- .Who

This is for the tasks elated to the person such as family members, colleagues, co- workers, boss, friends, cousins, relatives etc.

- .Active Projects

This tag is for all the projects that are active and being carried out currently. You must add this tag to things that are ongoing and need immediate attention.

- .Inactive Projects

These are projects that are inactive and not being carried out currently. They are for those that are yet to be finished.

- Read/Review

This tag is for all the things you need to read and review. It can include newsletters, emails, eBooks etc.

These form the various common tags that get used in Evernote and you can use these to have everything neat and organized and get things done faster and in a better way.

Chapter 6: Evernote Business

Now that we looked at all the various ways in which you can use the Evernote app to help better your life, let us now look in detail, at the "Evernote Business" app and explore its many facets.

As the name suggests, the app is designed for business purpose and features different uses as compared to the general Evernote app.

The Evernote business app is different from the regular Evernote app. You can specifically look for it in the app store.

The business app can be downloaded at a charge of 10$ a month and is specifically designed for business owners.

Many people confuse this with the Evernote premium app but these two are completely different. In fact, you can think of the ever note business app as the Evernote premium app for groups. But they are different and you need to buy this in order to use it.

The Evernote business app was released as a means to unite all the various facets of the business and bring the workforce together. After they realized that the regular app was not serving as an effective business oriented one, the company decided to build and release a business specific one.

It is meant to establish a free flowing communication base amongst all levels of the workforce including the staff and line.

The app will allow the various employees to use the app to communicate with each other, share the various information and also come up with new ideas to help better their business.

The app is easy to install and can be installed within a matter of seconds, thereby eliminating having to wait long hours to have it completely functional.

Let us now look at the various functions of the app and how it will help you in your business.

- One of the biggest and most useful functions of this app is that, your employees can avail cloud storage and also collaborate on various projects, which can be availed on various devices. So there is no wastage of time in going through files or looking for them to share them. Everything will be available in just one place and there will be no need to have various different systems in place.

- When it comes to office software's, one of the main concerns that people have is security. But with the Evernote business app, security should not be a cause for concern as the app provides extreme security and can also be used as a means to keep important data and files safe. The company works 24 hours to make sure that no security is breached as they have big companies in their list of clients and any breach can get them into big trouble.

- The second cause of concern when it comes to office software is that, people worry about the ease of use and how the new software will be perceived. As a solution to this very problem, there is an option for you to call up an expert and have him/ her guide you to install the app and also tell you of how successfully you can implement it in your business. You can hold a team session and help everybody understand how the app functions. They will anyway be aware of the Evernote app and here, they will only have to learn about the new added features.

- When it comes to business, there needs to be a clear line of communication between the employees, in order to be able to effectively collaborate on the various projects. The Evernote business app makes sharing extremely easy. It is possible for someone sitting in America to share their work with someone in

London. It is extremely easy to send data across to anybody no matter where they are. This feature is what makes the Evernote business app a boon to those who need to communicate with colleagues who are scattered all over the world. The employees can all seamlessly share the various projects and make it available to anyone in the company. At the same time, they can also lock their work, in case they fear theft of ideas.

- Another cause of concern is software's ability to undertake bulk operations and provide a smooth and problem free work environment. The Evernote business app has been built with utmost care and will not crash often. Even if it does (very rarely), it will make sure that no information is lost and everything is safely maintained in its backup systems. So you need not worry about losing anything or fear not having any data available when you urgently need it.

- One of the biggest advantages of this app is, how easy it is to use and how it will effectively make your work easier. The app will help you save on time and be able to spend the same time in a better way. Your team will progress faster and get more things done within a short period of time. The company will make steady progress and this will be a good thing for everybody involved including the employees and the bosses.

- There will also be the concern of how all the various platforms can be unified and data can be made available on all devices. But it is extremely easy to sync it and just like the Evernote app, it can be downloaded on all platforms and devices.

These form the generic benefits of the app let us now look at the various specific benefits.

The app has specific features that are to be used by specific groups in the business. For example: they have features that are meant to be utilized by people in the sales team, the real estate team, the customer care center etc. These are explained in detail as under:

- There is a particular function in the app, which is meant for use by the sales team. The feature will help the team maximize their sales potential and also allow them to maintain copies of all their sales records.

- The app is designed in such a way that, a free-flowing and smooth communication can be established between buyers and sellers. The various employees can successfully communicate with each other and avoid any miscommunications, as will the various buyers and sellers who will come together to conduct trades.

- The app can be used to build new content and also edit existing ones. It is also possible to have multiple copies including original and edited ones.

- One feature of the app that is widely appreciated is how it will allow you to create and store a knowledge bank for your company. So you can access any information from any point in time, no matter how far back, and use it to your advantage. Forget having to go through old dusty records, all you have to do is look up the records and find whatever you are searching for.

- The app is designed to help you conduct timely research and put out the best possible work. Like the general app, you can avail a safe Google search option and look for any detail on the web.

- The Evernote business app will help you in bringing together the various aspects of your business and also harmonize all the various functions in an orderly fashion. It is possible for you to remain as organized as possible in your work space and make the most of your efforts at work.

- Apart from the employees being in touch, the app will also help in getting in touch with the customers and help establish a smooth communication system with them. Records of the various interactions can be established and stored. They can be easily retrieved at any time and used for reference purposes.

- One other amazing feature of the Evernote app is that, it can be used as a marketing tool for your business. It can be used to market your business and also help you promote the various features in a specific and different manner.

- The cloud storage feature will allow everybody to avail their own and other's works just with the click of a single button. Your work related data can be accessed from any device and at any time and you don't have to wait to log into your office systems to look at it.

- The app will also allow for offline features, just like in the case of the general Evernote app. In fact, the features will be on par with the premium version of the app. So you can easily work on things when you are travelling. This can be a boon to those who have long flights and wish to make the most of their time by working on projects.

- This feature is especially useful for people who need to make changes in their existing files and or add new content to it. The files will also be available offline on the various devices that have been synced. And it is extremely difficult to do these if a particular app insists on having an internet connection. Given the amount of travelling that businessmen do, they can easily use this app in flights, in hotels, in countries without Wi-Fi connections etc.

- The business app also features a convenient work chat option, which will allow everybody to chat and share their ideas. It will allow you to share files and other data freely and make for smooth operating. You can have a different chat window or have a single one.

- You can talk and work at the same time, as the chat feature will not cause any type of hindrance.

-

Let us now look at the wonders of the presentation mode

The Evernote presentation mode is especially designed for businessmen and office goers, who showcase several presentations a day.

The feature is also useful for students but given the type of setting and aspects that it features, it is more useful for office presentations.

You can customize your presentations by changing the background, font, color etc. you can also change the color schemes and layout depending on the type of presentation that you wish you make.

Apart from the layout, you can also change the modes. There are two modes that are available, namely, the night mode and the day mode. The two come in shades of dark and light pastels.

The mode will allow you to add and edit any form of multimedia including images, videos, files etc. you can annotate over them just like you would over pictures and files in the general app.

Another advantage of the presentation mode is that, you can create a handy table of contents and add a link to each page. That way, you will not waste time looking for a particular page and can easily access it directly, just by clicking on it.

You can also make smaller presentation pages by putting links of images. By clicking on it, you can jump to an image and jump back to a page, thereby increasing the amount of written content on a page.

And since everything is synced, you can present the files from any device of your choice.

You can also open the presentation mode in a separate tab and have the regular Evernote app open, in case you need to make references to any of your other notes.

Apart from the annotating, you can also make use of the laser pointer. The laser pointer will allow you to point to all the important points on the screen. You can avail the feature by using a mouse.

To exit the presentation mode, you can simply hit the "Escape" button and close the presentation.

These form the wonders of the ever note business app and you can make use of it to increase your productivity at work.

Now that we have looked at each and every aspect of the ever note business in detail, we will now look at some of the newer features that were introduced recently.

Help with Evernote business

If you ever have any doubts to clear or want information on Evernote business then you can find answers to your questions on the Evernote support page. There are several questions that have all been answered and are meant to help you understand the concept better.

If at all you have a question that is not present or has not been answered satisfactorily then you can submit a question and wait for one of the experts to get back to you. This will ensure that all your doubts have been cleared. But it will take some time for the expert to have a look at you question and submit the right answer and if you are in a hurry then you can start a live chat to avail assistance from one of the helpers available online.

It is now possible for you to unify your Evernote app and your Evernote business app. There is a feature to place all your documents in one place and make sure that they are bifurcated. If you have a problem managing two different apps then simply unify them and place everything together in one app. You can separate your personal documents from your business and not have your colleagues peek into the former.

Don't worry, as your company will only have access to your business notebooks and not your personal notebooks. They can access, modify and delete your business notebooks but not your personal ones. This feature is a boon to the company as they have a bigger control over the notebooks and don't have to wait for an employee to authorize access to the business notebook. They can also add in data that will help the user and mass modify all the notebooks at once to save time and effort.

You can centralize your company's know how! All you have to do is connect your app with the company's business app and you will get a list of co-workers who are present in your company. You can go through each one's profile, look at what they are up to etc. and get a clear picture of where they stand. You can also easily exchange all the data with this feature. If you are looking for someone in particular then you can simply type in their name and search. Even if yours is a multinational company and has people all over the world then you can easily look for them without having to worry about finding out their details.

You can add in a new co-worker with ease. Simply send them an invite and get them on board. Everybody can have equal access to the notebooks and can modify it as and when they like. Inducting a new person can not only be simple but also allow them to get acquainted with the others by going through their profiles and looking at what work they are doing. If someone is trying to join in then you can either activate auto approval or a manual one if you think that unknown people or wrong people are trying to join in.

You can now easily separate each co-worker and collaborate individually with them. You don't always have to involve the entire group and can share knowledge and documents with just the chosen few. Apart from your group and a few, if you wish to showcase your work to the entire company then that is also a possibility. You can share your work with everyone present in the company and not have to shoot out individual mails to them.

The app will automatically synchronize all your related notes. This will ensure that you don't have to look for something that is related to your work and it will show up easily thanks to the synchronization.

You can look at all related notes that are present not only in your Evernote business app but in the entire company's app.

It is now possible for you to lock a document and share, which is an added security feature on the improved version. This was not a feature before and if security is a concern for you then this feature will help you in a big way. All you have to do is secure it with a password and the other person who knows the password can open it and not anybody. This might be important if you are sharing data in a group that need not go through everything that you share and it will save the other person a lot of time and effort.

Don't worry about your data getting leaked as Evernote has a team of experts who make sure that the firewall facilities are up to date and nobody outside the company can touch what you have shared with the company and co-workers.

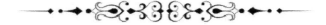

CONCLUSION

Thank you again for purchasing this book!

I hope this book was able to help you to learn everything about Evernote. If you were following along with the book, I hope by now you've gotten at least a little bit of confidence using Evernote. And I also hope that I've ignited at least a few ideas in your brain as to how to manage your life.

Remember that ever note is for everybody and you need not be a whizz to use it. Once you have a basic understanding of how things work, you will have the chance to use it with ease and make the most out of your life.

The next step is to start using Evernote deeply and thoroughly. Evernote is such a tool that the more time you invest in it, the more returns you'll get on your investments. Once you get in the habit of recording all information in Evernote, you'll see how powerful it can be. You'll realize that it truly feels like an extension of your brain. And the best thing is that you can use it in any way you want!

Use your own creativity to find the best ways to use Evernote and manage your life and your day to day time to increase your productivity and achieve success in life.

Finally, if you enjoyed this book, then I'd like to ask you for a favor, would you be kind enough to leave a review for this book on Amazon? It'd be greatly appreciated!

Thank you and good luck!

M.J. Brown

Check Out My Other Books

Here is a preview of my most popular book:

"Social Media Marketing"

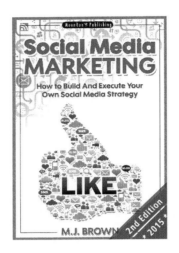

Chapter 1

A Crash Course on Social Media Marketing

The internet has become the main focus of all marketers. Print and TV advertisements now point to the website and social accounts of the company. The entire marketing campaign for any company, no matter how big or small, is tied around the company's web presence. But why is this so?

Just think about how many people are connected to the internet today. Almost the entire consumer base is present online and it spends a lot of time online. The mobile phone revolution shrunk the entire world into a globalized society and the advent of smart phones has connected the entire world by bringing the internet in the palms of our hands. There are more than a billion users just on Facebook.

The numbers alone are baffling but now think about what these people do on the internet. They connect with family, friends, strangers and colleagues, and they talk about their lives. They share jokes, news, photographs and videos. And they talk about products. Every marketer will tell you that the best type of marketing is "word of mouth" marketing.

When you hear about a product from someone you personally know, you automatically have more trust than if you were watching an advertisement on television. Social media marketing results in this type of word of mouth publicity that has a much bigger impact on prospective consumers than any other form of marketing. It also has the possibility of growing exponentially by going viral.

We've all heard about viral videos that reached millions of viewers in a few days. This potential to go viral is also why all marketers now focus a lot of social media.

So What Actually IS Social Media Marketing?

Social media marketing is a way of gaining traffic to your website through the use of social media sites. Marketing efforts in this area tend to concentrate on creating content that attracts the attention of their chosen audience and encouraging them to share it with all their friends and followers across social media. The result is an electronic word of mouth that spreads fast, earning the marketer good media visibility for next to no outlay.

Social media websites work by letting people interact with each other and build up relationships. When a business joins in, it allows potential customers to interact directly with them, creating a more personal touch and ensuring that customers are likely to pass the word about you on to their friends and families. And, because they are sharing your news with their friends, more people get to see it and pass it on to their friends, and so on, resulting in an increase in traffic that may convert to sales.

Social media marketing is used by more than 70% of today's businesses and has resulted in an increase of more than 130% in revenue. But it isn't only computers that are used for this; mobile phones and tablets are now used much more for accessing social media websites than they ever have been. Most smartphones have social media enabled and people are notified immediately when anything happens on their social media sites. This is a constant connection that allows businesses to keep their customers fully in the loop about what's happening and what's new.

Social Media Strategies

There are two main strategies that businesses should use with social media marketing:

The Passive Approach

Social media is a very useful source of information and customer voices for business. There are plenty of places where people share their views and their brand recommendations and business owners can tap into these and look at what the customer wants. In this sense, social media marketing is a cheap way of tapping into market intelligence, which is then used by the business to track down problems and opportunities. Let's take an example – the iPhone 6 Plus, released in September 2014.

The internet boiled over with videos of the newest handset from Apple undergoing a bend test after it was alleged that the handset could be bent by hand. This created no small amount of confusion amongst those who had been waiting for months for this new iPhone to be launched. Did Apple ignore it? No. They came straight back with a statement to say that this was a rare occurrence and they uploaded video shot in their own torture room, showing the iPhone 6 being put through a rigorous series of tests. As you can see, social media can now be used to get a live reaction to a product or service, making it extremely useful to any marketer.

The Active Approach

We can also use social media as a channel of communication and a way of engaging the public. There are quite a few companies who use some kind of dialogue online to build relationships with their customers, including the likes of Jonathon Swartz, CEO and President of Sun Microsystems and Bob Langert, Vice President of McDonalds. The idea is to encourage people to express their views, their ideas and pass on suggestions and using influences like this can be an extremely cost effective method of marketing.

The first requirement is to have an online presence. Whether you are a big company or a small startup, whether you are part of an organization or an individual, you need to have an online presence. Online presence simply means to set up shop in the virtual world. Think of it as a shop, a store, an office, or even a virtual basement that you work out of. This will be a website or a blog. This is the place where you'll send all your customers to find out more about your products or services and to buy what you are selling.

Along with a website, you need to be active on at least a few social networks. There are thousands of networks to choose from but you should only use as many as you can manage properly. There are the good old social networks such as Facebook, Twitter and Google+. There are video sharing sites such as YouTube and Vimeo. There are picture sharing sites such as Pinterest and Instagram. There are sites like Reddit, Scribd, Slideshare that allow you to curate and share other form of content. The type of product or service you are selling and the type of content you can create, will dictate the type of social network that you use.

Go where your audience is. Create what your audience wants.

Once you have the basic setup of a website/blog and a few social networks you can start engaging with people. Here's where the difference from traditional marketing starts. Unlike traditional marketing, this is not a one way communication channel. You can't just broadcast promotional content all the time and not interact with your audience. If you try to do this, you'll soon drive everyone away.

Instead, in social media marketing you need to listen to what others are saying. You need to have real communication with your audience. And most importantly, you need to provide real value to your audience. It's not "buy my product and you'll receive this much value." It's more like "here's all this free value for you and if you want more you can buy my product."

If you can understand this "catch" of social media marketing, then you'll be able to fully utilize it.

A lot of traditional marketers get into social media with their old habits. They only focus on building numbers and promoting their products endlessly to these numbers. They opt for quantity over quality. This approach doesn't work on social media and can actually have a negative effect. You should focus on quality instead of quantity. Even if you have a few hundred followers but all of them are dedicate fans of your product, you are in a much better situation than someone who has a hundred thousand followers but none of them really care about the product.

You can use tools for analyzing your social media outreach and see the kind of impact different content has on your audience. This ability to analyze your data is unique to social media marketing and it can prove to be very powerful. You can then tailor your content to suit exactly what your audience wants.

1. What Can You Do With Social Media?

If you have an online presence and are active on a few social networks and have a quality audience you can do the following things:

1. **Sell your products to your audience.** This is the main goal of any type of marketing.

2. ...

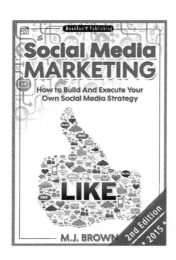

YOU CAN FIND THIS BOOK ON AMAZON NOW

Printed in Great Britain
by Amazon.co.uk, Ltd.,
Marston Gate.